JAMBOREE

Rhymes for All Times

JAMBOREE

Rhymes for All Times

Eve Merriam

Illustrated by Walter Gaffney-Kessell

Introduction by Nancy Larrick

A Yearling Book

Published by
Dell Publishing Co., Inc.
1 Dag Hammarskjold Plaza
New York, New York 10017

The poetry in this collection first appeared in THERE IS NO RHYME FOR SILVER, IT DOESN'T *ALWAYS* HAVE TO RHYME, CATCH A LITTLE RHYME, and OUT LOUD.

Yearling ® TM 913705, Dell Publishing Co., Inc.

ISBN: 0-440-44199-4

Printed in the United States of America

First printing—November 1984

CW

for Jonah

CONTENTS

GROWNUPS   66–67

"When parents are polite to you and say 'Please,'
It comes out soft as cooked green peas."

SPACES AND PLACES   80–81

"If I could go exploring,
Boldly I'd set forth"

INTRODUCTION

A jamboree is a frolic, a festival. A time for fun. For playing and singing and dancing.

Usually we think of a jamboree or festival as an occasion when people gather to take part in all kinds of fun and games. There may be jugglers and musicians over here, donkey rides for the children over there, country music, Popsicles and pizza pie for sale, clowns who paint children's faces, and hucksters galore.

Now Eve Merriam brings us a festival of poetry called *Jamboree: Rhymes for All Times*. It has all the excitement, variety, and fun of the song-and-games kind of festival that is an occasion. Instead of wandering from booth to booth on foot, you can roam through the pages and find entertainment of all kinds. You may encounter an alligator on the escalator or a bilgewater frog or even Ollie's polly-bird, all adding to the jamboree music that comes surging through the pages.

You'll hear the squawking baby, the ice-cream man (you vote for vanilla), and the circus band—*oompah, oompah*!

You'll meet the Optileast and the Pessimost, King Solomon ready to strike up a conversation, and a stray cat that wins your heart.

They reach out to you as they talk and sing, for this is a jamboree, which means everybody is in the act. You too.

You don't need a ticket. Or a passport. Or a costume. Nothing like that. You just need an appetite—an appetite for new foods, real adventures, tongue twisters that set you giggling, gentle words that stir the butterflies deep inside you.

From the list of poems—pages vii to viii—pick a poem that intrigues you: "Alligator on the Escalator" perhaps, or "The Stuck Horn." Then read your poem out loud even though you may be the only one to listen. Like a song, a poem is meant to be heard. On the printed page it is silent, waiting for someone to sing the melody, to give it the perfect sound.

Eve Merriam is a master of sound. She revels in made-up words ("Snickles and podes,/Ribble and grodes") and loves to juggle familiar words just for the fun of it:

> It jiggles, it joggles,
> it's juicy, it's jamful,
> it's a jester, a jockey . . .

Occasionally she will tell you to drag out a certain musical sound with a torrent of letters. (There are 155 O's in "The Stuck Horn," and you can hear why.) I scarcely need add that Eve Merriam loves to make us laugh—sometimes a great guffaw, but often a surprising little twist that sneaks up on us before we know it.

Her mood varies—sometimes teasing, sometimes "soft and purry." So, as you read, your tone of voice will change to suit the poet's change of mood. Now it is honking with "The Stuck Horn." Now scolding in "Company Manners." Now bamming and slamming with the steel wrecking ball.

Soon you will want to find a partner to read aloud with you—one to read Mr. Tall, the other Mr. Small, for example. Or one of you can read the words of the baby-sitter, the other the squawks of the baby in "The Baby-sitter and the Baby." Sometimes sound effects add to the fun: *Dot a dot dot, dot a dot dot* done with a tapping pencil for "Weather," or humming a gentle lullaby while "Night Song" is read.

As Eve Merriam puts it: There are

> Rhymes to whisper, rhymes to yell,
> Rhymes to chime like a swinging bell.
> Rhymes like a jump rope, now let's begin:
> Take a turn and jump right in.

Enjoy the jamboree!

—Nancy Larrick

THERE IS NO RHYME FOR SILVER

There is no rhyme for *silver,*
but if you climb a hill ver-
-y very slowly
you can almost make it go . . . See?

In the meanwhile, here are rhymes
For all seasons and all times.
Rhymes to sing and shout in Spring,
Rhymes to call out in the Fall.
Rhymes that leap in rocket space,
Rhymes that run around home base.

Fat and thin rhymes, tall and short rhymes,
Out and in rhymes, school and sport rhymes.
Hard as rocks, soft as cheese,
Rhymes that tickle, rhymes that tease.
Rhymes for when you're feeling quiet,
For times you'd like to make a riot.
Crazy, lazy, twirling, hurling,
Rhymes for reasons and for none—
Mainly just for having fun.

Rhymes at endings, rhymes in middles,
Jokes and twisters, puns and riddles.
Cold as glass, warm as fur,
Rhymes that prickle, rhymes that purr.
Dark rhymes, light rhymes,
Day and night rhymes,
You'll find odd and even verses
Including a couple of useful curses.
Rhymes to whisper, rhymes to yell,
Rhymes to chime like a swinging bell.
Rhymes like a jump rope, now let's begin:
Take a turn and jump right in.

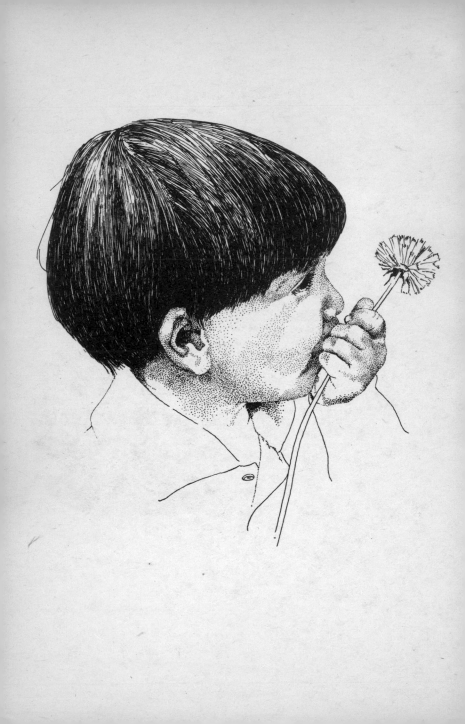

Weather and Seasons

Yellow, yellow, hello, yellow:
Welcome to forsythia and dandelions in Spring . . .

A YELL FOR YELLOW

Yellow, yellow, hello, yellow:
Welcome to forsythia and dandelions in Spring,
To buttercups and goldenrod and warblers on the
    wing.

Yellow, yellow, mellow yellow:
Yellow as new wood, yellow as wheat,
Yellow as cornbread sweet to eat.

Yellow, yellow, let's bellow yellow:
Yellow monkeys peeling bananas!
Yellow chickens playing pianos!
Butterflies, goldfish, cats' eyes!

Yellow, yellow, yell on yellow:
Yellow is a lemon smell, it tingles like a sneeze,
Tickles like the sunshine, jingles like a breeze!

SPRING FEVER

Danny dawdles
Sally shilly-shallies
Lloyd loiters
Guy gambols
Sylvia saunters
Peter procrastinates
Amanda meanders
Leonard lingers
Samuel ambles
Dorothy dallies
Harry tarries
and Molly lolls.

SUMMER RAIN

A shower, a sprinkle,
A tangle, a tinkle,
Greensilver runs the rain.

Like salt on your nose,
Like stars on your toes,
Tingles the tangy rain.

A tickle, a trickle,
A million-dot freckle
Speckles the spotted rain.

Like a cinnamon
Geranium
Smells the rainingest rain!

A COMMERCIAL FOR SPRING

Tired of slush and snow and sleet?
Then try this dandy calendar treat!

You'll like the longer, king-size days;
You, too, will sing this season's praise.

It's the scientific sunshine pill
(Without that bitter winter chill).

It's naturally warmer, it's toasted through,
Exclusively mild for you and *you*.

It comes in the handy three-month pack:
March, April, May—or your money back.

So ask for S-P-R-I-N-
G, you'll never regret it;
Remember the name, it's headed for fame:
Be the first on your block to get it!

AUTUMN LEAVES

Down
  down
    down
Red
  yellow
    brown
Autumn leaves tumble down,
Autumn leaves crumble down,
Autumn leaves bumble down,
Flaking and shaking,
Tumbledown leaves.

Skittery
Flittery
Rustle by
Hustle by
Crackle and crunch
In a snappety bunch.

Run and catch
Run and snatch
Butterfly leaves
Sailboat leaves
Windstorm leaves.
Can you catch them?

Swoop,
Scoop,
Pile them up
In a stompy pile and
Jump
   Jump
      JUMP!

THE SAPPY HEASONS

In the skue-bly sprays of ding
When yaffodils are dellow,
And tragnolia mees are mellow;
Then I feel a fively lellow,
Fively lellow.

In the good old tummer-sime
When lovers spike to loon,
And molden is the goon;
Then I hum a tappy hune,
Tappy hune.

When the autumn teaves are lurning
And there's lost upon the frand,
Still Thanksgiving's hose at cland;
So I'm feeling grimply sand,
Grimply sand.

When the winter blorms are stowing
And the snow is hiling pigh,
And nothing dreems to sy;
Then I'm glad that ug am snI,
Ug am snI.

IN THE NIGHT

Snow came in the night
Without a sound.

Like a white cloud tumbling
Down to the ground.

WEATHER

Dot a dot dot   dot a dot dot
Spotting the windowpane.
Spack a spack speck   flick a flack fleck
Freckling the windowpane.

A spatter a scatter   a wet cat a clatter
A splatter a rumble outside.
Umbrella umbrella umbrella umbrella
Bumbershoot barrel of rain.

Slosh a galosh   slosh a galosh
Slither and slather and glide
A puddle a jump a puddle a jump
A puddle a jump puddle splosh
A juddle a pump aluddle a dump a
Puddmuddle jump in and slide!

LULLABY

Purple,
Purple,
Twilight
Shy light.

Purple as a king's cape,
Purple as a grape.

Purple for the evening
When daylight is leaving.

Soft and purry,
Gentle and furry,
Velvet evening time.

Purple,
Purple,
Sky light
Goodbye light.

Dusky
Musky
Into night.

NIGHT SONG

Hushaby, hushaby, hushaby,
On velvet hooves the horses
Of darkness are riding on by.
Hushaby, hushaby, hushaby,
Galloping over the velvet sky.
> *Close your eyes and within the stillness*
> *You will hear the silent tune*
> *Of the spinning of the planets*
> *And the circling round of the moon.*

Hushaby, hushaby, hushaby,
On velvet wings the swallows
Of darkness are flying on high.
Hushaby, hushaby, hushaby,
Feathering over the velvet sky.
> *Close your eyes and within the stillness*
> *You will hear the silent tune*
> *Of the spinning of the planets*
> *And the circling round of the moon.*

Hushaby, hushaby, hushaby,
On velvet waves the dolphins
Of darkness arise from the deep.
Hushaby, hushaby, hushaby,
Sleep . . . sleep . . . sleep.

Close your eyes and within the stillness
You will hear the silent tune
Of the spinning of the planets
And the circling round of the moon.

Animals

Psst, psst.
Feel the kitten's silken fur
and hear her
soft as velvet
purr.

KITTY CORNERED

Psst, psst.
Feel the kitten's silken fur
and hear her
soft as velvet
purr.
Softly, softly,
purr, purr, purr.
Purr, purrrrrrrrrrr.

Grrrrrr.
The kitten doesn't want to play,
not today.
Grrr, grrrr.

Psst, little kitten,
don't run away.
Let me stroke your fur.
Softly, softly,
Purr, purr, purr.

Meow, not now.
Meow, meow.
MEOW!
NOT NOWWWWWWWWWWWW!

OLLIE'S POLLY

Ollie
has a polly-bird.
The only word
that bird can say
all the livelong
night and day
is

Quiet!
  Quiet!!
    Quiet!!!

When neighbors call to stop that riot,
Ollie's polly shouts back
QUIET!

TWO FROM THE ZOO

There is an animal known as a skink,
And no matter what you might happen to think
Or ever have thunk,

A skink—
Unlike a skunk—
Does not stink.
A skink is a skink.

If you go to the zoo
It may be on view
Alongside an aye-aye.

Aye, yes, that's right.
It's quite a sight.
Please take my word
That an aye-aye is not a sailor bird
Or anything else just as absurd.

No, it's truly
And zooly
A creature there.
Don't be afraid, since it's dulcet and docile
And not in the least
An unruly beast.

THE CAT SAT ON THE MAT

Did you ever know a cat
That sat on a mat?

The cats I have seen
Don't sit and preen.

They frisk and they tease,
They scramble up trees,
They tickle my knees,
They tangle in string,
They pounce and they spring,
They howl, yowl, and quiver,
And gobble up liver.

ULULATION

With a bray, with a yap,
with a grunt, snort, neigh,
with a growl, bark, yelp,
with a buzz, hiss, howl,
with a chirrup, mew, moo,
with a snarl, baa, wail,
with a blatter, hoot, bay,
with a screech, drone, yowl,
with a cackle, gaggle, guggle,
with a chuck, cluck, clack,
with a hum, gobble, quack,
with a roar, blare, bellow,
with a yip, croak, crow,
with a whinny, caw, low,
with a bleat, with a cheep, with a squawk, with a
    squeak:

animals
    —and sometimes humans—
                        speak!

ANIMALIMERICKS

1. Beware!

When a cub, unaware being bare
Was the best-dressed state for a bear,
Put on a barrel
For wearing apparel:
His mother cried "This I can't bear!"

2. An Odd One

There once was a finicky ocelot
Who all the year round was cross a lot
Except at Thanksgiving
When he enjoyed living
For he liked to eat cranberry sauce a lot.

3. Variety

A chameleon, when he's feeling blue,
Can alter his glum point of view
By changing his hue
To a color that's new:
I'd like to do that, wouldn't you?

A FISHY SQUARE DANCE

Tuna turn,
flounder round,
cuttlefish up,
halibut hold;

clam and salmon
trout about,
terrapin,
shrimp dip in;

forward swordfish,
mackerel back,
dace to the left,
ide to the right;

gallop scallop,
mussel perch,
grunion run,
bass on down;

finnan haddie,
skate and fluke,
eel and sole,
shad and roe;

haddock, herring,
hake, squid, pike:
cod promenade
and lobster roll!

ALLIGATOR ON THE ESCALATOR

Through the revolving door
Of a department store
There slithered an alligator.

When he came to the escalator,
He stepped upon the track with great dexterity;
His tail draped over the railing,
And he clicked his teeth in glee:

"Yo, I'm off on the escalator,
Excited as I can be!
It's a *moving* experience,
As you can plainly see.
On the moving stair I go anywhere,
I rise to the top
Past outerwear, innerwear,
Dinnerware, thinnerwear—
Then down to the basement with bargains galore,
Then back on the track to the top once more!
Oh, I may ride the escalator
Until closing time or later,
So tell the telephone operator
To call Mrs. Albert Q. Alligator
And tell her to take a hot mud bath
And not to wait up for me!"

CHEERS

The frogs and the serpents each had a football
   team,
And I heard their cheerleaders in my dream:

"Bilgewater, bilgewater," called the frog,
"Bilgewater, bilgewater,
Sis, boom, bog!
Roll 'em off the log,
Slog 'em in the sog,
Swamp'em, swamp'em,
Muck mire quash!"

"Sisyphus, Sisyphus," hissed the snake,
"Sibilant, syllabub,
Syllable-loo-ba-lay.
Scylla and Charybdis,
Sumac, asphodel,
How do you spell Success?
With an S-S-S!"

THE STRAY CAT

It's just an old alley cat
that has followed us all the way home.

It hasn't a star on its forehead,
or a silky satiny coat.

No proud tiger stripes, no dainty tread,
no elegant velvet throat.

It's a splotchy, blotchy
city cat, not pretty cat,
a rough little tough little bag of old bones.

"Beauty," we shall call you.
"Beauty, come in."

Children

If I could have
Any wish that could be . . .

WISHING

If I could have
Any wish that could be

I'd wish that a dog
Could have me.

<u>SUPPOSE</u>

Suppose I covered up my mouth:
I couldn't sing, I couldn't shout;
I couldn't whistle like a tea-kettle spout.

I couldn't pretend I'm a baby and cry,
Or ask over and over *Why, why, why???*

I'd have to grunt like a pig,
Or snort like a horse.
I'd have to keep all my giggles in.

Though of course

I could keep secrets
And I still could grin.

SUPPOSE AGAIN

If I held on to my nose,
How could I smell a rose?
Or burning leaves,
Or a lawn fresh mowed,
Or the musty fust
Of a dusty road?

Or cinnamon buns,
Or hardware stores,
Or orange peels,
Or sawdust floors?

Well, I suppose
I won't hold my nose.

Still, there is one vegetable
I'd just as soon not smell.
(Cauliflower! Glub!)

A VOTE FOR VANILLA

Vanilla, vanilla, vanilla for me,
That's the flavor I savor particularly
In cake or ice cream
Or straight from the bean
In pudding, potatoes, in fish or in stew,
In a sundae, a Monday, the whole week-long
   through!

I care not a sou, a hoot, or scintilla,
A fig or a farthing—except for vanilla!
Boo, foo, eschew sarsaparilla;
More, adore, encore vanilla!
From the Antarctic to the Antilles,
Vive Vanilles!

On the first of Vanilla I'll write to you,
At half-past vanilla we'll rendezvous;
By the light of vanilla we'll dance and we'll fly
Until vanilla dawns in the sky.
Then to a vanilla villa we'll flee
By the vanilla side of the sea,
With vanilla tables, vanilla chairs,
Vanilla carpeting on the stairs,
Vanilla dogs, vanilla cats,
Vanilla shoes, vanilla hats,
Vanilla mice in vanilla holes,
Vanilla soup in vanilla bowls:

Vanilla, vaniller, vanillest for me,
The flavor I favor most moderately!

SATELLITE, SATELLITE

Satellite, satellite,
The earth goes around the sun.

Satellite, satellite,
The moon goes around the earth.

Satellite, satellite,
I have a little satellite:

My little brother orbits me
And pesters day and night.

51

SOMETIMES

Sometimes I share things,
And everyone says
"Isn't it lovely? Isn't it fine?"

I give my little brother
Half my ice-cream cone
And let him play
With toys that are mine.

But today
I don't feel like sharing.
Today
I want to be let alone.
Today
I don't want to give my little brother
A single thing except
A shove.

PECULIAR

I once knew a boy who was odd as could be:
He liked to eat cauliflower and broccoli
And spinach and turnips and rhubarb pies
And he didn't like hamburgers or French fries.

MILLIE AND WILLIE

When
Millie and Dottie and Lottie
And Rita and Carmencita
All play ball
And Willie wants to play, too,
And they say
"Go away, you're a boy.
"Go jump in the lake, bellyache!"
Then
Don't you agree with Willie
That girls are stupidly silly?

But
When Willie and Freddy and Teddy
And Juan and Don
Play ball
And Millie wants to play, too,
And they say
"Go away, you're a girl.
"Go tell your mother she wants you,
You big fat skinny dunce you!"
Then
Don't you agree with Millie
That boys are stupidly silly?

PETE'S SWEETS

Pete
will eat
anything
if it's sweet.

Peppermint soup,
or ice cream on toast.

Though what he likes most
is a jelly sandwich
without any bread.

Or instead,
a bubble-gum chop.
Chew your meat thoroughly, Pete.
"I am. Cancha hear me?" *Pop!*

A MATTER OF TASTE

What does your tongue like the most?
Chewy meat or crunchy toast?

A lumpy bumpy pickle or tickly pop?
A soft marshmallow or a hard lime drop?

Hot pancakes or a sherbet freeze?
Celery noise or quiet cheese?

Or do you like pizza
More than any of these?

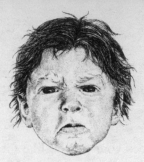

MEAN SONG

Snickles and podes,
Ribble and grodes:
That's what I wish you.

A nox in the groot,
A root in the stoot
And a gock in the forbeshaw, too.

Keep out of sight
For fear that I might
Glom you a gravely snave.

Don't show your face
Around any place
Or you'll get one flack snack in the bave.

GOING TO SCHOOL

Going to school
I pass a street
where there is a hardware store
and next to it
a flower shop.

I like to stop
and greet
the flowers on display,
then see next door
different kinds of blooms:
bright paint cans,
shiny pots and pans,
a bouquet
of mops and brooms.

A NUMBER OF NUMBERS

One is a number that may be conceited,
That thinks of itself as sweet honey or jam:
For one is the number of people I am.

Two is the usual number for shoes.
Is it because one's too easy to lose?

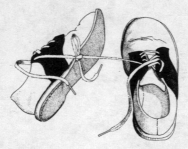

Half circle and then a half circle again.
Though *three* feels it's boring to be so repeated,
Still, it is far better off incompleted.
For if its two halves into one whole were caught,
Then all that is three would amount to just naught.

Four makes the legs for a table or chair.
It can do the same thing for a tiger or bear.

Five is a highway going straight and then
It takes a sharp left and turns right round again.

Six is a cherry with a long stem;
In summer I eat any number of them.

Seven is the edge of a ship out at sea;
You can't see the captain, for he's taking tea.

Eight is a number of which I am fond;
It goes skating in circles over the pond.
It's also a double top you can spin,
Or a very fat cat with its tail tucked in.

Nine is the full moon caught up in a tree:
Will somebody tall please release it for me?

ASSOCIATIONS

Home to me is not a house
Filled with family faces;
Home is where I slide in free
By rounding all the bases.

A tie to me is not
Clothing like a hat;
It means the game is even up
And I wish I were at bat.

QUIBBLE

U can be seen without a Q.
But Q must always go with U.

I think it's queer
And not quite right.

So here is a Q all on its own.
Come on, Q. Stand up alone.
U keep out.

Alas, poor Q feels qivery, qavery,
Qietly sick . . .

Hurry back, U,
To the rescue—quick!

CATCH A LITTLE RHYME

Once upon a time
I caught a little rhyme

I set it on the floor
but it ran right out the door

I chased it on my bicycle
but it melted to an icicle

I scooped it up in my hat
but it turned into a cat

I caught it by the tail
but it stretched into a whale

I followed it in a boat
but it changed into a goat

When I fed it tin and paper
it became a tall skyscraper

Then it grew into a kite
and flew far out of sight . . .

THE OPTILEAST AND THE PESSIMOST

The Optileast
Is a cheerful beast;
The least little thing
Makes his joy-bells ring.

The Pessimost
Is given to boast
That there's always room
For more and more gloom.

Now these two creatures, queer to relate,
Whom nature would scarcely be able to mate;
Who neither the other could ever abide,
Who surely could never live side by side—
Queer as can be, although they're not kin,
They dwell within the very same skin.

Times when my Optileast is here,
My Pessimost does not appear,
And yet he's somewhere down below
Even though he does not show;
So do not be alarmed or shout
If he should suddenly break out.

Then when my Pessimost is seen
And acting bigly mean as mean;
Without any warning in advance,
My Optileast begins to dance:
The smallest flower, or nothing at all,
Can make him leap up laughing tall.

Strange Optileast and Pessimost,
Neither is guest, neither is host;
They couldn't be brothers, they couldn't be wed,
Yet they'll live together until they're dead.
For however peculiar it may be,
They're both alive, alive in me.

HURRY

Hurry! says the morning,
Don't be late for school!

Hurry! says the teacher,
Hand in papers now!

Hurry! says the mother,
Supper's getting cold!

Hurry! says the father,
Time to go to bed!

slowly, says the darkness,
you can talk to me. . . .

Grownups

When parents are polite to you and say "Please,"
It comes out soft as cooked green peas.

MANNERS

When parents are polite to you and say "Please,"
It comes out soft as cooked green peas.

But when they get angry and they still say "Please,"
Then it sounds more like a sneeze.

PULLEEEAAAZZZE!

CONVERSATION

"Buenos días," says Señor Rías.
"Bonjour," says Monsieur Dutour.
"Buon giorno," says Signoro Tiorno.
"Hello," says Mister Coe.

"Buenas noches," says Señora Rochas.
"Bonne nuit," says Madame La Brie.
"Buona notte," says Signora Capolotte.
"Good night," says Mrs. Whitc.

"Hasta luego," says Señorita Diego.
"Au revoir," says Mademoiselle Loire.
"Arrivederci," says Signorina Terci.
"See you soon," says Miss Calhoun.

COMPANY MANNERS

Hands off the tablecloth
Don't rumble belly
Don't grab for grub
Don't slurp the soup
Don't crumble the crackers
Don't mash the mushrooms
Don't mush the potatoes
Don't stab the steak
Don't slap the saltshaker
Don't pill the bread
Don't swill the sauce
Don't ooze the mayonnaise
Don't slop the slaw
Don't spatter the ketchup
Don't gulp the olives
Don't spit the pits
Don't finger the lettuce
Don't dribble dressing
Don't chomp the celery
Don't gobble the cobbler
Don't guzzle the fizz
Swallow, don't swig
Don't smack your lips
Pat with a napkin
Daintily dab
Quietly quaff
Fastidious sip
And gracefully sample
A nibbling tidbit.

TO MEET MR. LINCOLN

If I lived at the time
That Mr. Lincoln did,
And I met Mr. Lincoln
With his stovepipe lid

And his coalblack cape
And his thundercloud beard,
And worn and sad-eyed
He appeared:

"Don't worry, Mr. Lincoln,"
I'd reach up and pat his hand,
"We've got a fine President
For this land;

And the Union will be saved,
And the slaves will go free;
And you will live forever
In our nation's memory."

WHICH WASHINGTON?

There are many Washingtons:
Which one do you like best?
The rich man with his powdered wig
And silk brocaded vest?

The sportsman from Virginia
Riding with his hounds,
Sounding a silver trumpet
On the green resplendent grounds?

The President with his tricorne hat
And polished leather boots,
With scarlet capes and ruffled shirts
And fine brass-buttoned suits?

Or the patchwork man with ragged feet,
Freezing at Valley Forge,
Richer in courage than all of them—
Though all of them were George.

TEEVEE

In the house
of Mr. and Mrs. Spouse
he and she
would watch teevee
and never a word
between them spoken
until the day
the set was broken.

Then "How do you do?"
said he to she,
"I don't believe
that we've met yet.
Spouse is my name.
What's yours?" he asked.

"Why, mine's the same!"
said she to he,
"Do you suppose that we could be—?"

But the set came suddenly right about,
and so they never did find out.

THE BABY-SITTER AND THE BABY

Hush hush hush the baby-sitter sighs
waw! waw! waw! the little baby cries
Hush Hush shh shh Hush Hush Hush
   wawawwawwwwwww
     hush hush
       waw waw
        hush hush
         WAW!
Ah ooh ooh the baby-sitter tries
snuggle you and huggle you gently ooh ah ooh
Naw naw naw the baby cries and cries
  hush hush
    waw waw
      ooh ooh
       NAW!
Lulla lulla lulla lull you lullabys
sleepy sleepy sheepy
deepy dreamy lullabys
please will you please please please shut your eyes
YiYiYi the baby cries and cries
  hush hush
    waw waw
      ooh ooh
       naw naw
        lulla lulla
         yi yi
        yi
  yi
 YI!

A LAZY THOUGHT

There go the grownups
To the office,
To the store.
Subway rush,
Traffic crush;
Hurry, scurry,
Worry, flurry.

No wonder
Grownups
Don't grow up
Any more.

It takes a lot
Of slow
To grow.

MR. TALL AND MR. SMALL

Said Mr. Tall to Mr. Small,
"I see a skyscraper,
And a kite flying high
Made of crimson paper."

Said Mr. Small,
"I don't see any such things at all.
But I do see a ball
Rolling away behind a wall."

Cried Mr. Tall,
"Look what I found—
A bird's nest up in the old elm tree!"

Replied Mr. Small,
"As for me,
I just found an acorn on the ground."

"The top of a mast,"
Espied Mr. Tall.
"Caboose chugging last,"
Vied Mr. Small.

"Upon my word,"
Announced Mr. Tall,
"There's a giraffe."

"Don't be absurd,"
Pounced Mr. Small,
"It's a baby calf."

"Flagpoles," said Mr. Tall.
"Moles," said Mr. Small,
"In holes."

Said Mr. Tall,
"I see clouds that pass
All billowing pink,
Like a pillow for sleep."

Said Mr. Small,
"I'll take, I think,
A nap on the grass,
Green velvet deep."

KING SOLOMON

King Solomon was such a wise old king
That people came to ask him everything.
They asked questions that would baffle you or me,
But Solomon could answer them—one, two, three!

    "Solomon, King Solomon, you're such a wise man,
    Try to answer this question if you can!

"What's the happiest music to be heard?
Is it the song of the nightingale bird?
The quivering note of a violin string?
A silver bell with a golden ring?
A piano playing a thunderous note?
An accordion that folds like a paper boat?
A merry-go-round at a county fair?
A circus band in the village square?

"We will cross deserts and climb mountains, too,
In search of the answer we seek now from you."

King Solomon smiled: "You needn't roam,
For the answer you seek is close to home.

"The happiest music to be heard
Is not the song of the nightingale bird,
The quivering tone of a violin string,

A silver bell with a golden ring,
A piano playing a thunderous note,
An accordion that folds like a paper boat,
A merry-go-round at a county fair,
A circus band in the great town square—

"No, the happiest music that there can be
Is a boy or girl whistling in an apple tree!"

"King Solomon, King Solomon, then tell us true
The answer to the second riddle we ask of you:
What is the strongest ship that can sail
That won't bend or break in the stormiest gale?"

Solomon thought for a moment or two,
Then he said, "The ship for me and for you
That will hold calm and steady to the end of the trip
Is the one that we share best—it is good friend-ship."

"Solomon, King Solomon, you're such a wise man,
Answer this last riddle if you can:
What's sweeter than sugar or jam or honey
And what you can't buy for barrels of money?"

Solomon looked low, Solomon looked high,
First down at the ground, then up at the sky;
The sun was like a daffodil yellow and bright,
And a blade of April grass was dancing in the light.
"Oh, sweeter than sugar or jam or honey,
And what you can't buy—not for barrels of money,
Is the sweetest treasure that nature can bring:
That after winter there always comes spring!"

Spaces
and
Places

If I could go exploring,
Boldly I'd set forth

EXPLORING

If I could go exploring,
Boldly I'd set forth
With Ponce de Leon in Florida,
With Lewis and Clark in the North.

I might go with Magellan
And sail around the Straits,
Or with Marco Polo to Asia
And the Chinese gates.

With Hannibal I'd cross the Alps,
With Caesar into Gaul,
With Leif Ericson to Greenland;
But I'd like best of all

To be on the Santa Maria
Or Niña or Pinta that day
When Christopher C. came sailing
Into the New World bay.

SPACE SONG

Jupiter, Saturn, Uranus, Mars;
Here we go whizzing around the stars.

Venus, Neptune, Mercury,
And oh, Pluto—
What on Earth do you see?

How little Earth looks down below:
What tiny creatures they must grow!

BAM, BAM, BAM

Pickaxes, pickaxes swinging today,
Plaster clouds flying every which way.

Workmen are covered with white dust like snow,
Oh, come see the great demolition show!

Slam, slam, slam,
Goes the steel wrecking-ball;
Bam, bam, bam,
Against a stone wall.

It's raining bricks and wood
In my neighborhood.
Down go the houses,
Down go the stores,
Up goes a building
With forty-seven floors.

Crash goes a chimney,
Pow goes a hall,
Zowie goes a doorway,
Zam goes a wall.

Slam, slam, slam,
Goes the steel wrecking-ball;
Bam, bam, bam,
Changing it all.

GEOGRAPHY

You can ride for long treks
In *Tex*. and *New Mex*.

Skyscrapers high
In *N.Y*.

Fish
In *Mich*.

Tomatoes in *N.J*.
Flowers in *Va*.
Coal in *Pa*., and rice in *La*.

Cotton in *Ala*.
Okra in *Okla*.

Corn grows in *O*.,
Mo., and *Io*.

Lumber in *Minn*.
In *Mont*. there's tin.

Chickens in *R.I*.
Cattle in *Wy*.
Hunter's pie in *Ky*.

Fla. beaches,
Ga. peaches.

Wash. grows pears,
Col. has bears.

Shoes come from *Mass.*,
Salmon from *Alas.*

Cal., redwood trees,
Wisc. is known for cheese.

Mushrooms in *Del.*
Conn., Christmas trees to sell.

Kan. sows wheat,
Ill. ships meat.

Green hills in *Vt.*
Now that's enough from *Me.*

Seventeen states more I leave
For *U.* to abbrieve.

A RHYME IS A JUMP ROPE

A rhyme is a jump rope—
Let's begin.
Take a turn and
Jump right in.

What can we do with a rhyme for *today*?

Perhaps we'll go sailing in the *bay*.
We could feel the silver dots of *spray*.
We might watch the white gulls fly *away*.

In Turkey a king is known as a *bey*.
In Paris there's a street called Rue de la *Paix*.
Olé in Spanish means the same as *hooray*.

How long do you think this rhyme will *stay*?
Until the sky turns dark and *gray*?
(If you were a horse you could answer *neigh* . . .)

A JAMBOREE FOR J

It's hard to make a *j*
sound anything but joyful:
it's jubilant, it's jocund,
it joins in a jig.
It japes, it jibes, it jingles,
it jitterbugs, it jets.
It jangles, it jumps rope,
it jounces in a jeep.
It jiggles, it joggles,
it's juicy, it's jamful,
it's a jester, a jockey,
a jaunty jackanapes.
It's a juggler, a jouster,
a jar full of jellybeans,
it's a julep, a jujube,
a jocose jinni,
a journey in a jolly boat—

by jeepers, by jiminy,
by Juno and by Jupiter,
what jovial high jinks!

SOUVENIR

I bring back a shell so I can always hear
the music of the ocean when I hold it to my ear:

then I feel again the grains of sand
trickle sun-warm through my hand

the sea gulls dip and swoop and cry
as they dive for fish then climb the sky

the sailboats race with wings spread wide
as the wind spins them round and they glide ride glide

my lips taste a crust of salty foam
and sandpipers skitter and crabs scuttle home

where I build a castle of Yesterday
that the high tide washes away away

while I keep the shell so I can always hear
the music of the ocean when I hold it to my ear.

SCHENECTADY

Although I've been to Kankakee
And Kalamazoo and Kokomo,
The place I've always wanted to go,
The city I've always wanted to see
Is Schenectady.

Schenectady, Schenectady,
Though it's hard to pronounce correctly,
I plan to go there directly.

Schenectady, Schenectady,
Yes, I want to connect with Schenectady,
The town I select is Schenectady,
I elect to go to Schenectady,
I'll take any trek to Schenectady,
Even wash my neck for Schenectady,
So expect me next at Schenectady,
Check and double check
Schenectady!

THE STUCK HORN

unmOOOOOOOOOOOOOOving
in glUUUUUUUUUUUUUUUUUe

sunk in OOOOOOOOOOOOOOOOOOze
snaggling in the same dragging
grOOOOOOOOOOOOOOOOOOOOOOOOOOOve

throw a bOOOOOOOOOOOt or a shOOOOOOOOOOOe
gag it with a rag bottle it stopple it pickle it
pinprick it tickle it with a straw from a
brOOOOOOOOOOOOOOOOOOOOOOOOOOOm

just when you think it will stop it
reneWWWWWWWWWWWWWWWWWWWWWWWWWWs

somebody please
dOOOOOOOOOOOOOOOOOOOO
something sOOOOOOOOOOOOOOOOOOOOOOOOOOOOOOOn

CIRCUS

The circus is coming to town!
The brass band plays OOmpah OOmpah
Thumpa thump
Thumpa THUMP
Thumpa OOmpah OOmpah *pow*.
Get your ticket
get your ticket
the Big Show's beginning right *Now*.
Get your popcorn
get your program
get your root beer and frankfurter here.
The tent goes up goes *up* goes UP,
the sawdust ring is spread,
get a grandstand seat—hey, *down* in front,
we can't see over your head!
The lions growl in their cages,
the tamer cracks his whip,
oompah thump   oompah thump
the bears dance, the elephants prance,
oompah thump   oompah thump
a poodle pulls a cart with a cat,
a rabbit jumps from a black top hat,

TIME

a parakeet whistles *Dixie*
and drinks from a paper cup.
Thumpa thump.
Trapezes fly, your heart goes skip
as a bicycle climbs the high wire
oompah thump   oompah *thump.*
Acrobats tumble and leapfrog,
spangles and tightropes and spotlights,
a leotard lady, a leopard-skin man,
and a giant baby who lifts a van
OOOMP!
And watch him fall down, the comical clown
with the conical hat and the pom-poms
the chalk-white cheeks and the cherry-red nose
and the horn that blows
and the hidden hose
that squirts water wherever he goes.
Honk!
The circus is coming to town.
OOmpah *honk!*
The circus is coming to town.
HONK!

93

MNEMONIC FOR SPELUNKING

From the cavern of my mind
Here's a remembrance clue
That was passed along to me,
Now I pass it on to you:

Stalactites from the ceiling show;
Stalagmites from the ground up grow.

WHERE IS A POEM?

Where is a poem?
As far away
As a rainbow span,
Ancient Cathay,
Or Afghanistan;

Or it can be near
As where you stand
This very day
On Main Street here
With a poem
In your hand.

What makes a poem?
Whatever you feel:
The secrets of rain
On a windowpane,
The smell of a rose
Or of cowboy clothes,
The sound of a flute
Or a foghorn hoot,
The taste of cake
Or a freshwater lake,
The touch of grass
Or an icy glass,
The shout of noon
Or the silent moon,
A standstill leaf
Or a rolling wheel,
Laughter and grief:
Whatever you feel.